THE 52 CHURCHES WORKBOOK

BECOMING A SPIRITUAL COMMUNITY THAT MATTERS

VISITING CHURCHES SERIES

PETER DEHAAN

The 52 Churches Workbook: Becoming a Spiritual Community that Matters

Copyright © 2019 by Peter DeHaan.

Visiting Churches Series

All rights reserved. No part of this book may be reproduced, disseminated, or transmitted in any form, by any means, or for any purpose without the express written consent of the author or his legal representatives. The only exception is short excerpts and the cover image for reviews or academic research. For permissions: PeterDeHaan.com/contact.

Published by Rock Rooster Books

ISBN:

978-1-948082-35-8 (e-book)

978-1-948082-36-5 (paperback)

978-1-948082-37-2 (hardcover)

Credits:

Developmental editor: Cathy Rueter

Copy editor: Robyn Mulder

Cover design: Cassia Friello

Author photo: Chele Reagh / PippinReaghDesign

To all spiritual seekers looking for a place to belong and all churches that want to be that place.

Books in the Visiting Churches Series:

52 Churches

More Than 52 Churches

Visiting Online Church

Shopping for Church

The 52 Churches Workbook

The More Than 52 Churches Workbook

For a list of all Peter's books, go to PeterDeHaan.com/books

CONTENTS

The Beginning   1

GETTING STARTED

Church #1: A Friendly Place with a Homey Feel   5
Church #2: Growing Deeper, Not Wider   8
Church #3: It Only Hurts When You Care   11
Church #4: Successfully Melding Contemporary and Traditional   14
Church #5: Catholics are Christians Too   17
Church #6: A Quintessential Country Church   20
Church #7: The New Church   23
Church #8: A Grand Experiment   26
Church #9: Methodists Know How to Cook   29
Church #10: A Special Father's Day Message   32
Church #11: Charismatic Lite   35
Church #12: More Methodists, More Food   38
Church #13: A Dedicated Pastor Team   41
Part One Perspective   44

THE SECOND QUARTER

Church #14: The Pentecostal Perspective   49
Church #15: An Outlier Congregation   52
Church #16: Something's Missing   55
Church #17: A Doubleheader   58
Church #18: Revisiting Roman Catholicism   61
Church #19: A Near Miss   64
Church #20: Different Language, Same God   67
Church #21: A New Kind of Church   70
Church #22: A Caring Community   73
Church #23: They'll Be Fine   76
Church #24: Good but Not Typical   79
Church #25: Embarking on a Metamorphosis   82
Church #26: An Unknown Situation   85
Part Two Perspective   88

THE HALFWAY POINT

Church #27: A Charismatic Experience	93
Church #28: Intriguing and Liturgical	96
Church #29: Led by Laity	99
Church #30: Misdirected and Frustrated	102
Church #31: A Day of Contrasts	105
Church #32: Commitment Sunday and Celebration	108
Church #33: A Shepherd Cares for His Flock	111
Church #34: Acts Chapter Two	114
Church #35: A Well-Kept Secret	117
Church #36: The Surprise	120
Church #37: Another Small Church	123
Church #38: A Refreshing Time	126
Church #39: A Great Way to End the Year	129
Church #40: No Time to Return	132
Church #41: People Make the Difference	135
Church #42: High Expectations and Great Disappointment	138
Church #43: A Welcoming Church with Much to Offer	141
Church #44: A Familiar Place	144
Part Three Perspective	147

THE HOME STRETCH

Church #45: Another Doubleheader	151
Church #46: False Assumptions	154
Church #47: Significant Interactions	157
Church #48: Small, Simple, and Satisfying	160
Church #49: Large and Anonymous	163
Church #50: Saturday Mass	166
Church #51: The Megachurch: A Grand and Welcoming Experience	169
Church #52: Playing it Safe	172
Church #53: Home for Holy Week	175
Part Four Perspective	178
Reflections	180
A Lot Like Dating	182
Greeting Well or Not at All	184
Format and Size Matters	186

Candy's Take on 52 Churches	188
Generalizations	190
Tips for Improvement	192
Conclusion	195
The Visiting Churches Series	197
About Peter DeHaan	198
Books by Peter DeHaan	199

THE BEGINNING

What started as a desire to learn more about nearby churches morphed into a much bigger vision. At God's prompting, I planned an unconventional faith journey, one of adventure and discovery. My goal was to learn what he would show me by visiting a different Christian church every Sunday for a year.

My wife, Candy, served as my faithful accomplice throughout the whole thing. We eventually called our sojourn "52 Churches."

Some people thought we were crazy. We were. Others thought we were brave. We weren't. Any courage came from our dependence on God each step of the way.

Each week I blogged about our experience. Readers wanted more.

Then I wrote a book: *52 Churches: A Yearlong Journey Encountering God, His Church, and Our Common Faith*. Readers still asked for more.

This book is the first step in providing more: more information and more insight. This workbook is a guide to discovering key truths from *52 Churches* that we can apply to our local branches of Jesus's church.

Note that *52 Churches* is a narrative that celebrates the good we experienced when visiting churches, along with some recommendations for improvement. To be of maximum value, this workbook, however, focuses on the items needing correction. This isn't to denigrate the churches we attended, but to serve as a guide to move *all* churches into a more effective outreach.

Use this book in whatever way benefits you the most. It might be for personal introspection, a small group or Sunday school class discussion starter, or as a guide for church leadership to reform church practices for greater kingdom impact.

As we move forward to contemplate and respond to this workbook, we can become a church that matters to our community and advances the good news of Jesus.

But whatever you do, don't let this book collect dust. Read it, contemplate it, and apply it. Then give God the glory for the results.

Amen.

GETTING STARTED

I'm preparing to go to Church #1. The enemy harasses me. I don't want to go. I now understand why the non-regular church attender can so easily stay home despite their best intentions. The living room recliner and television remote are much more inviting and much less threatening.

Welcoming visitors starts before they arrive. *What can you do to make it easy for them to show up?*

A personal invitation is the most effective way to encourage people to visit your church. *What specific things can you do to invite people to visit?*

CHURCH #1: A FRIENDLY PLACE WITH A HOMEY FEEL

This church has no online presence, as well as an uninviting exterior. But the people inside are friendly, and we feel at home—mostly.

An unwieldy wheelchair ramp tacked onto the front of the building desperately needs painting. We bypass the ramp, but it remains our focal point and forms our first impression. *What changes should you make to give your church better curb appeal and offer a better first impression?*

A man lacking in social skills, with possible mental issues, corners us when we arrive. We can't escape his plodding monologue. *What can you do to protect visitors from regular attendees who may repel or scare them away?*

There are only seventeen people present. With a smirk, the minister asks first-time visitors to raise their hands. I want to disappear. *What practices should you stop so that people won't squirm?*

_____

_____

_____

_____

_____

_____

_____

_____

After the service, everyone lingers to chat. Many thank us for visiting and invite us to come again, but they aren't pushy. *What can you do to help a person's first visit not be their last?*

_____

_____

_____

_____

_____

_____

_____

_____

CHURCH #2: GROWING DEEPER, NOT WIDER

The church is three years old and meets in a strip mall. Their goal is to "grow deeper, not wider." Everything about this church is the opposite of last week.

I park near the door. I later realize they leave the prime spaces for guests, with the regulars parking further away. *When you arrive at church, where do you park and why?*

_____

_____

_____

_____

_____

_____

_____

_____

Scores of people mill about, all engaged in conversation. We mosey in, giving time for someone to notice us. No one does. We sit and squirm in silence. *Who do you talk to before church: friends, regulars you don't know well, or visitors? Why? What needs to change?*

_____

_____

_____

_____

_____

_____

_____

_____

Despite singing and hearing a message, most of the service relates to church business. *How can you address church business and still make it meaningful for new people? Should Sunday mornings have an external focus, saving internal discussions for a different time?*

_____

_____

_____

_____

_____

_____

_____

_____

Although they ignored us after we walked in, the overall atmosphere and service was much more welcoming than last week. I want to come back. *What can you do to make it easy for people to engage in your service and want to return?*

_____

_____

_____

_____

_____

_____

_____

_____

CHURCH #3: IT ONLY HURTS WHEN YOU CARE

The third church is more established like Church #1 but more midsized like Church #2.

Many pages on their website are "under construction" or "coming soon." The sections for members have information, while the pages for visitors are incomplete. *What can you do to keep your website up-to-date and relevant for visitors?*

_____
_____
_____
_____
_____
_____
_____
_____

Finding the church is a person's first challenge. Knowing which door to enter is next. This facility has several doors, all unmarked. We don't know which one to use. *How can you better guide people to the correct entrance?*

_____
_____
_____
_____
_____
_____
_____
_____

These folks dress up for church. I don't. My appearance doesn't bother me, but it might be a problem for others—both visitors and members. *Will visitors who dress differently feel comfortable at your church or out of place?*

___

As we walk in, a friend spots me. She says, "This won't be a typical service." One of their members died by suicide. The service will address their loss. *If your service will have unexpected content or be difficult to deal with, what can you do to alert guests to help them avoid unpleasant surprises?*

CHURCH #4: SUCCESSFULLY MELDING CONTEMPORARY AND TRADITIONAL

This church's Facebook page—they have no website—says their "services are informal with a blend of hymns and contemporary music."

I suspect the service will match what I see in the facility, a merging of traditional and contemporary, just as promised online. *Does your church deliver what you promise? If not, what needs to change?*

_____

_____

_____

_____

_____

_____

_____

_____

_____

We sit only a third of the way in, yet most people pack in behind us. *Where do you sit in church? Why? Many visitors like to sit toward the back to remain anonymous. What can you do to leave room for them?*

_____

_____

_____

_____

_____

_____

_____

_____

_____

Some people raise their hands in worship as we sing, yet most don't. I want to, but I fear calling unwelcomed attention to myself if I do. *How can you help people feel comfortable in worshiping God at your church?*

Afterward, they invite us to stay for coffee and cookies. So many people talk to us that snack time is over before we reach the fellowship hall. *How can you avoid being in such a hurry to pick up that guests feel rushed or shortchanged?*

CHURCH #5: CATHOLICS ARE CHRISTIANS TOO

When I tell people we're visiting area churches, I specify *Christian*, but they often hear *Protestant*. It surprises them to learn we'll visit Catholic gatherings too. Today is our first.

A flurry of last-minute and late arrivals distract me from the service. *When do you typically walk into church and why? How can you minimize distractions from latecomers?*

Throughout the morning, I'm pleased to see laypeople take part. *What can you do to involve more people in your service?*

The service is hard to follow. We never know what to say when a congregational response is required. We eventually discover some of this information in a book called the Missal, but it doesn't help much. *How can you help people navigate your church's traditions and practices?*

_____

_____

_____

_____

_____

_____

_____

_____

When the priest announces mass is over, the people dart out. They don't tarry to talk. *Does your church value community? What can you do to help people connect with each other?*

_____

_____

_____

_____

_____

_____

_____

_____

CHURCH #6: A QUINTESSENTIAL COUNTRY CHURCH

This small church didn't come up in our online research, but we have driven past it. All we know is their name and service time.

A wheelchair ramp suggests the way inside, but we're surprised when it doesn't lead to the main entrance. The small side door looks tightly shut. We retrace our steps in frustration. *How can you direct guests to the right entrance?*

___

Once inside, a lady hands us a bulletin and visitor card. The card is important to them. Three more people will offer us one before we leave. *How does your church gather information about visitors? How can you do it better?*

After a few songs, there's an extended greeting time, but we're boxed in and can't move. Given our lack of mobility, we can do nothing but smile awkwardly. *If your church has a mid-service greeting, what can you do to make it a positive experience for everyone?*

Many people invite us to stay afterward for refreshments. This is an extended time of community and celebration. They're happy to linger in one another's company. *How can you best embrace people in your after-church fellowship?*

CHURCH #7: THE NEW CHURCH

I suspect this church is only a couple years old. I later learn they're an outgrowth of a small group.

Their meeting space looks abandoned. We approach with uncertainty. I hesitate to walk inside. It wouldn't take much to make the entrance more inviting. *What simple things can you do to make your church building say "welcome" instead of "go away"?*

_____
_____
_____
_____
_____
_____
_____
_____

Inside, people mingle. Several introduce themselves in a friendly, unassuming way. They're great at pre-church interaction with people they don't know. *How can you best connect with visitors before church? How can you encourage others to follow your example?*

_____
_____
_____
_____
_____
_____
_____
_____

The 52 Churches Workbook

Their leader is a tentmaker pastor. Like Paul in the Bible, he works for a living to share Jesus for free. Without him drawing a salary, there is more money for outreach and ministry. *How might your church move away from depending on paid staff and tap the skills of capable volunteers?*

_____

_____

_____

_____

_____

_____

_____

_____

As is often the case, it's new churches—not established ones—where people are most apt to discover God and grow into a vibrant faith. *What can you do to promote a new-church excitement where you worship?*

_____

_____

_____

_____

_____

_____

_____

_____

CHURCH #8: A GRAND EXPERIMENT

This week we visit our third new church. It's a grand experiment, one quite radical from their conservative denominational roots.

A greeter welcomes us and explains what to expect during our visit. *How can you help visitors at your church know what will happen?*

_____

_____

_____

_____

_____

_____

_____

_____

We learn they hold Vacation Bible School in partnership with other area churches. I appreciate them working together. The high school also held their baccalaureate service here. *How can your church become more community-centered and less inward focused?*

_____

_____

_____

_____

_____

_____

_____

_____

At the concluding song, a man confuses everyone by coming forward to become a member, even though no one gave an invitation. As the band plays, some members take initiative to join him and start him on his journey. *Do you feel free to take initiative in dealing with unexpected situations? If not, what needs to change?*

For the first time, we don't have a chance to talk with the minister. I'm disappointed but not critical. It should be members who connect with visitors, not paid staff. *Whose job is it to interact with visitors at your church? How can you involve more people?*

CHURCH #9: METHODISTS KNOW HOW TO COOK

Today, we'll go to a United Methodist church, our first visit to a widely recognized denomination.

Their services are traditional. I wonder if I should dress up, but their website doesn't say. Though my casual attire is out of place, no one seems to object. *How do you react when someone shows up at church who looks or dresses differently from everyone else?*

We make our way inside. Two greeters hand out preprinted nametags to the regulars. They offer us stickers to write our names on. I find nametags helpful. *How can you use nametags to enhance community and celebrate guests?*

The minister is female. I applaud the opportunity for all people to use their gifts and skills to serve God in any capacity, including leading and teaching. *How do you react to women in leadership and ministry roles at your church?*

_____
_____
_____
_____
_____
_____
_____
_____

A closing number ends the service, and we make our way to the fellowship hall for a potluck. These Methodists know how to cook. *How does your church use a shared meal to enhance community?*

_____
_____
_____
_____
_____
_____
_____
_____

CHURCH #10: A SPECIAL FATHER'S DAY MESSAGE

Today's church has no website, and their Facebook page only links to their denomination's website.

With no online presence, their outreach efforts are nonexistent. Their future lacks promise. Members will die with no one to replace them. *What is your church doing to attract younger people?*

_____

_____

_____

_____

_____

_____

_____

_____

Their older building has an aged exterior, exacerbated by neglect. Grass grows through the cracks in the parking lot. Inside is more of the same. They've made updates but in a basic, we're-on-a-tight-budget, way. Regular attendees overlook these issues. Visitors do not. *What steps should your church take to have an inviting facility?*

_____

_____

_____

_____

_____

_____

_____

_____

Several members introduce themselves. We reciprocate, but no one bothers to engage in conversation. *Beyond introducing yourself, what else can you do to interact with others?*

A technical glitch leaves their retractable screen in the up position. The planned service relied on video. The pastor's message—which I suspect he quickly pulled together—celebrates God as a father to the fatherless. It goes smoothly and no one gripes. *When church services don't go as planned, how well do you adjust without complaint?*

CHURCH #11: CHARISMATIC LITE

The trendy website of this church gives no indication of their focus or affiliation. In contrast, their Facebook page says they're charismatic.

Despite their claim to be charismatic, their service is much like nontraditional evangelical churches. *If your church is to stand out, what are you doing that's truly different?*

According to their pastor, many of the people there dropped out of other churches, disillusioned and discouraged. This church became their sanctuary. *What can you do to embrace the disillusioned and discouraged?*

For the second time in two weeks, there's no effort to obtain our contact information. I'm not sure if this is good or bad. *Does your church attempt to get contact information from visitors? If so, what do you or should you do with it?*

___

Contrary to their self-description as charismatic, there was little in their service to support that claim. *Does your website and social media accurately reflect your church?*

___

CHURCH #12: MORE METHODISTS, MORE FOOD

Next up is another United Methodist Church. It's a rural church and not on the way to anywhere we go, so we didn't know it existed.

Their website is the most visitor-friendly site we've seen. Notably is a "what to expect" section, addressing the concerns a new person might have. *Does your website tell people what they can expect? What do you need to add to make your outreach more effective?*

_____
_____
_____
_____
_____
_____
_____
_____

We arrive to a full parking lot, as their website said might happen, but there are still a few spaces near the door, and we use one of them. *Where do guests end up parking at your church? How can you make it easier for them?*

_____
_____
_____
_____
_____
_____
_____
_____

Unlike our other church experiences, the minister clearly communicates their Communion procedure. I know what to expect. *Do you explain your practice of Communion in a way that embraces newcomers? How can you make this better?*

___

Several people invite us to stay for refreshments in the fellowship hall. We leave well-fed, both spiritually and physically. *How well does your church do at feeding people physically and spiritually?*

___

CHURCH #13: A DEDICATED PASTOR TEAM

This church has no website and a blank Facebook page. The lack of information online discourages me.

The pastor welcomes us warmly. He's expecting us because Candy emailed him to confirm service times. *What can your church do to make it easier for people to find you and feel welcomed?*

We sing the hymn, "No Other Plea." One line resonates with me, "My great Physician heals the sick. The lost he came to save." *Does your church promote Jesus as both healer and savior? How can you embrace a more holistic view of him?*

If not for family coming over, the pastor would have invited us to his home for lunch. I'm honored. Sharing a meal is a wonderful way to launch a friendship. *Should you invite church visitors to have lunch with you? What else could you invite them to do?*

_____

_____

_____

_____

_____

_____

_____

_____

Aside from the pastor and his wife, no one in the congregation makes any effort to talk to us. *Do you expect your minister to greet new people or should members do that as well? What role can you play in welcoming guests?*

_____

_____

_____

_____

_____

_____

_____

_____

PART ONE PERSPECTIVE

We're one-quarter of the way through our journey. It's been more than I'd hoped for and at the same time, not as much of what I expected.

Every church we visited had strengths we can celebrate. *What positive things would a visitor say about your church?*

_____
_____
_____
_____
_____
_____
_____
_____

And every church had weaknesses that need correcting. I'm just not sure if they're aware of these issues. *What criticisms might a visitor have about your church?*

_____
_____
_____
_____
_____
_____
_____
_____

THE SECOND QUARTER

The next thirteen churches promise a wider variety of experiences. This excites me. Our journey is about growth and discovery, not about thoroughly covering every option in a precise order.

We can experience a lot of variation from one church to the next. *When you visit a church, do you expect one just like yours or something different? Why?*

___

The local branches of Jesus's church are diverse. *How well do you do at accepting the diversity of Jesus's followers? How well does your church do?*

CHURCH #14: THE PENTECOSTAL PERSPECTIVE

The church website doesn't give their affiliation, but the pastor's bio implies they're Pentecostal. Their Facebook page, however, prominently confirms this.

Facebook says the service lasts two hours. Glad to know, I still dread what awaits me. *Most people expect church to last an hour. If yours doesn't, what can you do to communicate this without scaring away newcomers?*

_____

As posted online, their narrow views on salvation and unity trouble me. But most members don't know what their church stands for—and would disagree with some aspects. *How well do you know your church's beliefs? If we focus on Jesus, does doctrine really matter?*

Several more people welcome us. This church excels at pre-service hospitality, leaving us feeling valued. *What is your church noted for? Is it something positive or negative?*

_____
_____
_____
_____
_____
_____
_____
_____
_____

After we meet many people, the minister introduces himself and asks if we've ever been to a Pentecostal church. When I shake my head, he raises his eyebrows and requests we keep an open mind. *Do people at your church need to keep an open mind? What does this communicate?*

_____
_____
_____
_____
_____
_____
_____
_____
_____

CHURCH #15: AN OUTLIER CONGREGATION

Their website says we'll find "a laid-back, coffeehouse atmosphere" with "an unconventional setting where a blend of people, of all ages, from all walks of life, can gather and feel at home." This is my kind of church. It's an outlier congregation in a mainline denomination.

Weather permitting, the service will be outdoors. I'm excited for a chance to worship in nature, but I'm disappointed I won't experience their typical service. *Regular attendees may appreciate a special service, but how does this impact visitors?*

___

We arrive and see no hint of an outdoor service. We later learn that based on today's forecast for ninety-three degrees, they decided to meet inside. *How well does your church deal with last-minute changes?*

The service starts with a video. It's an allegory that shows the importance of churches maintaining their original purpose: focusing outward and avoiding the snare of self-centeredness or adopting an inward preoccupation. *How can your church better maintain an outward focus?*

_____

_____

_____

_____

_____

_____

_____

_____

_____

Next is a time for healing prayer, another first on our journey, and a most welcome one. *Does your church offer healing prayer for people in need? Do you?*

_____

_____

_____

_____

_____

_____

_____

_____

_____

CHURCH #16:
SOMETHING'S MISSING

This nondenominational church meets in a public school auditorium.

Renting space saves the church from purchasing and maintaining a facility. *Whether you own your building or rent space, how can you maximize your outreach and better impact your community?*

_____
_____
_____
_____
_____
_____
_____
_____

They use more technology than we've seen so far. When not displaying song lyrics, Bible verses, or clips, they project the pastor's video on a large screen behind him. *How much technology does your church use during your services? Does it add to or detract from the experience?*

_____
_____
_____
_____
_____
_____
_____
_____

Aside from a greeter and the two pastors saying "Hi," no one talks to us. We learn that people wearing green nametags are available to answer questions. After the service I spot a man with a green nametag, but he rushes by. *Are you and other people at your church so preoccupied or busy that you overlook and ignore people?*

_____

_____

_____

_____

_____

_____

_____

_____

The leadership at this church does the right things to foster spiritual connection, but the people aren't following. They're passive, coming to church, doing church, and then leaving. *Is it the paid staff's job to welcome visitors, or yours? What needs to change?*

_____

_____

_____

_____

_____

_____

_____

_____

CHURCH #17: A DOUBLEHEADER

This church has a contemporary service followed by a traditional one. We'll go to both.

Their idea of *contemporary* is vastly different from mine, with this service being one of the more reserved ones we've attended. *If you state a certain type of service, what do you need to do to better deliver on your promise?*

_____

_____

_____

_____

_____

_____

_____

_____

They provide a sign language interpreter for the hearing impaired, who sit in the first three rows. It's a treat to watch them sing with their hands and sign interactive portions of the service. *What can your church do to help those with various limitations better engage in worship?*

_____

_____

_____

_____

_____

_____

_____

_____

For communion, there's no invitation for nonmembers to partake. We decide that we shouldn't, but the usher motions us to go up. *Do people know what to expect when you serve communion? What can you do to include visitors and welcome them to participate?*

___

No one mentions it, but we find coffee and donuts in the fellowship area. Next to each is a donation basket. I feel guilty for grabbing a treat without feeding the fund. *What practices in your church would seem odd or off-putting to outsiders?*

CHURCH #18: REVISITING ROMAN CATHOLICISM

Today we visit our second Roman Catholic Church. I'm excited—and nervous.

The large sanctuary is grand without being ostentatious. Contemporary and airy, it seats several hundred. It's the largest we've seen so far. *Does your building facilitate worship or limit it? What needs to change?*

_____

_____

_____

_____

_____

_____

_____

_____

This Catholic Church seems even more steeped in ritual than Church #5. While they announce hymns, the rest of the liturgy proceeds without direction. We think we're prepared, but we aren't. *How can you help people better engage in your worship service?*

_____

_____

_____

_____

_____

_____

_____

_____

After the Eucharist is a ritual where we exchange the greeting "Peace be with you" to those around us. This is the only interaction we have with anyone the entire morning. The priest dismisses us, and the people scatter. *What can you do to interact with people at your church and foster community?*

_____

_____

_____

_____

_____

_____

_____

_____

I leave feeling empty. Though their traditions have meaning to those who understand them, it's a roadblock to visitors. *What can you do to help outsiders better follow your church's practices and not walk away empty?*

_____

_____

_____

_____

_____

_____

_____

_____

CHURCH #19: A NEAR MISS

With no website and a phone line that doesn't work, we assume this church, listed only in a computer-compiled online directory, either no longer exists or never did. The sign in front of their building is the only reason we know the service time.

When we arrive, a greeter welcomes us, but she's surprised to see two new people. *Are visitors the norm at your church or an exception? What needs to change?*

_____

At times their service seems evangelical and other times mainline, with hints of Charismatic. It's an ideal blend. *How can your church service better focus on Jesus instead of promoting a subset of Christianity or a denomination?*

_____

In the most insightful communion invitation I've ever heard, the pastor affirms that all who are in relationship with God are free to participate, regardless of church status or affiliation. *How inclusive and accepting are your church's practices?*

Their mission is to help people on their faith journey, connecting them with other churches that match their needs and preferences. It's okay if they happen to pick up members along the way, but it's not their intent. *What are your church's growth goals?*

CHURCH #20: DIFFERENT LANGUAGE, SAME GOD

This week is another doubleheader, but with a twist. First is a Mandarin worship service and English Sunday school, followed by an English worship service and Mandarin Sunday school.

We email to ask if non-Chinese are welcome. We are. Some non-Chinese attend the Mandarin service. *How well do you embrace people of different races and cultures?*

For worship, they display the words in Mandarin, with the English translation underneath. I read the words in English as I enjoy the melodic beauty of a different tongue. *How well can people who speak another language engage in your service?*

We don't see the minister until he stands to give the message—until now, the laity has led the service. Speaking in Mandarin, the minister is dynamic, animated, and at times funny. I laugh with everyone else even though I don't know why. *If people don't know your language, how might they perceive your nonverbal communication?*

Afterward several people invite us to stay for lunch. Sharing a meal is important to them. They do this every Sunday. *How important is sharing a meal at your church? In what other ways can you foster community?*

CHURCH #21: A NEW KIND OF CHURCH

Most of this church's ministry happens on Saturday. The Sunday service is for those they meet during their Wednesday evening street ministry.

We turn to Hebrews 6, but as the pastor begins her message, the Holy Spirit sends her to Ephesians 4. We never make it back to Hebrews. *How much do you depend on the Holy Spirit to lead your meetings? How willingly do you follow?*

_____
_____
_____
_____
_____
_____
_____
_____

Later, we discuss how the message applies to us. This mutual interaction is helpful, building community in the process. *What can you do to allow for more interaction to occur during church?*

_____
_____
_____
_____
_____
_____
_____
_____

Ninety minutes later we move into worship. The first song lasts twenty minutes. I kneel in reverence and then bow in awe of God. *How often does worship cause you to bow in reverence and awe? What's missing?*

___

If you view church in a traditional manner, then we didn't go today. If you understand church as two or more people gathered in the presence of God, then today offered much. *What are the essential elements for church to take place?*

CHURCH #22: A CARING COMMUNITY

This church meets in a newer, contemporary building. It's most inviting.

Many people introduce themselves. Their genuine interest, without being pushy, refreshes me. They ask our names, which they repeat with care. When they share theirs, they pause, giving us time to hear and remember. *How important are people's names to you and your church?*

The minister is losing his voice. After introducing the topic, he lets the congregation finish the message. He invites them to share their stories of what others have done for them, how they showed love, and provided care. The congregation does this well. *How well does your church do at sharing during a service? How can you do it better?*

This congregation is a genuine community. They prove it in the quiet ways they help each other. "Caring for community is a witness," says the pastor. *What is your church's witness? What is its reputation?*

_____

_____

_____

_____

_____

_____

_____

_____

After the service, the pastor excuses himself. He fades away, perhaps because he doesn't feel well, but more likely because he doesn't need to be there. The congregation envelops us into their community. *How well can your church function without your minister being present?*

_____

_____

_____

_____

_____

_____

_____

_____

CHURCH #23: THEY'LL BE FINE

Last Sunday was their minister's last day. Other area clergy have great respect for him. I wish I could have met him.

Today ends their summer schedule with one contemporary service. Next week they'll switch to their winter format with two services: one traditional and the other contemporary. Had we known, we might have come next Sunday for a doubleheader. *If your church has seasonal schedules, why? How does this impact people who want to attend your service?*

_____

_____

_____

_____

_____

_____

_____

_____

Like Church #8, the church's youth programs are part of Young Life, a nondenominational youth ministry, which taps college students as leaders. *What programs do you have that might be more effective if you worked with existing, external ministries?*

_____

_____

_____

_____

_____

_____

_____

Throughout the service, a person mills about, occasionally sitting and sometimes murmuring. She appears homeless and acts mentally ill. Though I'm distracted, I'm pleased no one confronts her behavior or shoos her from God's house. *How does your church treat those who don't fit in or act strangely?*

___

Afterward, two members confirm that their former minister prepared them to function without him. They expect to do just fine. *How well would your church function without a minister? How long could you keep it up?*

CHURCH #24: GOOD BUT NOT TYPICAL

This church resulted when three dying congregations merged a quarter century ago, but with a worship team of teens brought in, today isn't a normal service.

Most of the congregation are senior citizens, with few children. The sanctuary seats about four hundred, but it's only one-fourth full. *If you have an aging congregation, what can you do to reverse the trend?*

The absence of a cross is conspicuous. This isn't an issue for me, but for many it is. The cross is a prime emblem of Christian faith, but we must remember it's only a symbol. *What symbols are present or lacking in your church? What message might this convey?*

Today's sermon is about friendship. True friendship, the minister says, requires constancy, honesty, and wise counsel. Jesus is the ultimate friend. *How well do you do at being a true friend to others?*

___

Both before and after the service, people thank us for visiting. Their conversations aren't to share faith but to entice us back. They're desperate to grow. *How do your efforts to grow your church come across? Are you willing to ask a visitor their thoughts to get a firsthand account?*

___

CHURCH #25: EMBARKING ON A METAMORPHOSIS

The website of this church shows captivating photos of their worship team, implying high energy and an edgy sound.

Everyone wears an adhesive nametag, and we make our own. At some churches members wear permanent nametags and guests use temporary ones, which single them out. *If your church uses nametags, how can you best embrace others? If you don't use name tags, why not?*

_____
_____
_____
_____
_____
_____
_____
_____

Friends invite us to sit with them. Though we don't need this comforting gesture to feel welcome, a typical newcomer might appreciate it. *In what ways can you help a person feel more comfortable?*

_____
_____
_____
_____
_____
_____
_____
_____

The worship team is far different than their website portrays. Instead of a high-energy, edgy worship band, there's a laid-back team of two. I'm disappointed. *Is your website an accurate reflection of your services? If not, what do you need to change?*

However, this discrepancy between website and reality may be because in a few months this church will cease their Sunday meetings. They'll relaunch with another church to form a new group, with a new name, and a renewed focus. Change is hard, but these people anticipate it. *How can your church better deal with change? How can you help?*

CHURCH #26: AN UNKNOWN SITUATION

 friend tells us about a new African American church. Once again, we'll be minorities at church.

We arrive ten minutes early and find only four people. At ten o'clock there's just nine. A few more trickle in. Eventually the service begins. *Is your starting time a guideline or reality? What message does this send?*

_____

Everyone is friendly, abounding in smiles. Despite having different-colored skin, we feel accepted. *How can you better welcome people of different backgrounds at your church?*

_____

Throughout the service, the pastor declares blessings on us. His words are intentional and more fervent than I've ever witnessed. His passionate prayer proclaims favor, protection, and God's grace. This isn't a request but a declaration. I like his spiritual confidence. *How can you pray with more boldness?*

_____

_____

_____

_____

_____

_____

_____

_____

Afterward they share a meal. As Candy and I return to our chairs with our food, they congregate in groups. No one joins us or invites us to join them. I don't think they're being rude but merely gravitating toward their friends and those they're comfortable with. *What should you do to push past your comfort and reach out to include others?*

_____

_____

_____

_____

_____

_____

_____

PART TWO PERSPECTIVE

For the past twenty-six weeks we've sought to expand our understanding of how others worship God.

I now realize that church is not about the teaching or music. It's about community. *How can your church foster community and promote meaningful connections?*

_____

_____

_____

_____

_____

_____

_____

_____

Consumerism is rampant in today's church. People seek a church with the most engaging speaker and entertaining musicians. They stay until a better preacher or music comes along. They are church consumers, looking for the best value. *How can you move your church away from a consumer mindset?*

_____

_____

_____

_____

_____

_____

_____

_____

THE HALFWAY POINT

I've felt like we're bouncing between a rural culture to the west and a more metropolitan vibe to the east. Going forward, we'll plan our visits by geographic area, not driving distance.

I never expected such a noticeable difference between rural and more metropolitan churches. *Regardless of your location, how can your church better reflect your community?*

We changed plans because what we once did no longer works. Many churches need to embrace this reality and try something new, but they don't. *Where does your church need a new approach? Where should you maintain the status quo? Are you sure?*

CHURCH #27: A CHARISMATIC EXPERIENCE

This charismatic church meets in an old, run-down building, originally built for shared-tenant use. It looks abandoned and forms our first impression.

With a half dozen equally accessible doors, we don't know which one to use. Regular attendees know which entrance to head to; guests do not. *What changes should you make so that you don't hamper people from entering your church?*

_____

_____

_____

_____

_____

_____

_____

We sit and an unpleasant odor assaults me. I eventually grow to accept it, but I never like it. *What offensive smells and other distractions do you need to remove from your church? (And don't cover one smell with another.)*

_____

_____

_____

_____

_____

_____

_____

During their "testimony and prayer" time, each person who prays does so loudly, to the point of shouting. *How do your prayers come across?*

___

They encourage us to worship any way we wish, but during the sermon the minister chastises us: "Forty percent of you did not worship God today." He does indeed have expectations in how we worship, and he judged us as falling short. *What worship expectations does your church have? What needs to change?*

___

CHURCH #28: INTRIGUING AND LITURGICAL

We learn of this church when we spot their name in a local paper's church directory. Still, we struggle to confirm their meeting time.

We walk inside and a lady shares some basic information about the liturgy for today's service. Without her help, we'd have been lost. *Whether you're a liturgical church or not, how can you help people better navigate your service?*

_____
_____
_____
_____
_____
_____
_____
_____

During the sermon the minister forewarns us we will greet each other later with a holy kiss. Though there's only a handful of people, they're all strangers. This is the creepiest of practices. *What does your church do that may cause people to squirm? (And before you say nothing, think harder.)*

_____
_____
_____
_____
_____
_____
_____
_____

After the service they invite us to stay for fellowship. A neighbor and her dog join us. Though she missed the service, she's welcomed anyway. *How do you feel about people skipping church and showing up afterward to hang out?*

___

Even though it was hard to participate, some of this church's strange worship traditions fascinate me. *Do your church practices and worship intrigue others or push them away? How can you make your service more accessible?*

___

CHURCH #29: LED BY LAITY

s we pull into the church parking lot, we realize our daughter attended preschool here, many years ago.

We amble in and one woman approaches us and mutters to herself, "Where's the guest registry?" She moves toward an ornate wooden stand that holds nothing. As she searches for the missing book, I walk past her. *How ready is your church to receive visitors?*

_____

_____

_____

_____

_____

_____

_____

The minister is gone, and a member fills in. Though not an accomplished speaker, I applaud what she's doing. In fact, members lead the entire service. *Can your church hold a service without your minister or staff? If not, what should you do?*

_____

_____

_____

_____

_____

_____

_____

They invite kids to come forward for the children's message as music plays. Though the song is appropriate for preschoolers, the five who come forward are much older: later elementary through high school. *What traditions does your church persist in even though it no longer makes sense?*

_____

_____

_____

_____

_____

_____

_____

_____

During the message, someone passes us a clipboard with a sign-in sheet. I watch the clipboard weave its way in the rows ahead of us. I'm so distracted that I never reconnect with our speaker. *What church practices distract people from hearing the message and worshiping God?*

_____

_____

_____

_____

_____

_____

_____

_____

CHURCH #30: MISDIRECTED AND FRUSTRATED

When Candy asked about the service time, the pastor confirmed what their website said: 10 a.m. When we arrive, they tell us to sit anywhere. After fifty agonizing minutes they say, "Thanks for coming. The service will start in about ten minutes."

We just endured an agonizing Sunday school. They must think they're clever, but I feel manipulated. They should be honest and say church starts at eleven. *How might people feel tricked or misled about your church's practices or the information posted online?*

_____
_____
_____
_____
_____
_____
_____
_____

We sing old-time hymns with piano accompaniment. They sing with vigor. *How might people characterize the singing and worship at your church? Is their assessment acceptable?*

_____
_____
_____
_____
_____
_____
_____
_____

One man wears a lapel pin of the Baptist flag. He thinks his pin is a conversation starter, but his dogmatic discourse pushes me away. *In what way might our words, passion, or doctrine repel people?*

Today we heard a powerful message and worshiped God with people passionate about singing, but tricking us into attending Sunday school remains my key memory. *What parting memory do people leave with from your church? (If they don't come back, you made a bad impression.)*

CHURCH #31: A DAY OF CONTRASTS

This church offers a mix of old with new, contemporary with traditional, and public friendliness with personal indifference.

At one point, the leader asks everyone who is able, to kneel. It hurts when I kneel. So focused on my pain, I miss the prayer. *What practices in your church may get in the way of people encountering God?*

Two girls read about the Good Samaritan: the first in Spanish and the second in English. But this is the only bilingual part of the service. *What changes can you make to your service so it's more accessible to people of other languages or cultures?*

Afterward is a Thanksgiving potluck. Publicly, they invite all to join them, but no one personally does. "If we walk slowly," Candy says, "maybe someone will ask us to stay." No one does, so we leave. *What can you do to personally invite someone to do something?*

_____
_____
_____
_____
_____
_____
_____
_____
_____

Aside from the two greeters at the door, no one talks to us. After the service I try to make eye contact with many people, but fail each time. I don't matter and want to cry. *How can you let people know you care?*

_____
_____
_____
_____
_____
_____
_____
_____

CHURCH #32: COMMITMENT SUNDAY AND CELEBRATION

This church has been homeless for a while, but they moved into their own space last week. Today they celebrate God's faithfulness on a trying journey.

We learn it's commitment Sunday for them, with contribution pledges sought for the upcoming year. The woman who explains this is embarrassed that our first visit falls on their annual plea for money. *When you ask for money, how can you help visitors feel welcomed and not obligated?*

_____
_____
_____
_____
_____
_____
_____
_____

When their minister learns we're not used to liturgical services, she introduces us to someone who can guide us. He takes his job seriously and performs it admirably. *How can you apply this visitor-friendly gesture to your church services?*

_____
_____
_____
_____
_____
_____
_____
_____

The guest speaker says, "Bigger is no longer better in the church world," and "Smaller is where the work will be done." He's so right. *What is your attitude toward church size? Does something need to change?*

Afterward is a brunch to celebrate God's provision. "We don't want to intrude on your celebration," I say to one lady. Her response removes all doubt, "*You* are one of the reasons we're celebrating." *How well do you celebrate visitors?*

CHURCH #33: A SHEPHERD CARES FOR HIS FLOCK

Even though this church is only nine miles from our house, the contrast between their lives and mine is stark. These people live in poverty.

We struggle to sing hymns. The organist learned to play because no one else could, and the minister isn't adept at leading singing. We push through. God doesn't care about our musical ability, only our heart. *How can we better align our perspective with his?*

The people of this rural congregation struggle getting enough to eat. Behind the church is a sizable garden, planted for their church community. The pastor offers venison for Thanksgiving to those in need, as well as firewood to help heat their homes. *How open are you to see the needs of others? What can you do to help?*

The reality of these people's lives puts an exclamation point on being in need. *How can you help meet the tangible needs of the people in your church? Your neighborhood?*

_____

_____

_____

_____

_____

_____

_____

_____

These people worship God with their church community, their extended family. Being together is what matters. This minister takes care of his tiny flock. He loves them, and they, him. *How can you show love to others?*

_____

_____

_____

_____

_____

_____

_____

_____

CHURCH #34: ACTS CHAPTER TWO

Today's destination is a charismatic church. We've not been to many so I'm excited for the experience.

We arrive ten minutes early. With only two cars in the lot, my anticipation sags. We walk in, surprising six people who aren't expecting visitors—or anyone else. Yet Jesus says he will be there when two or more gather. *How can we better embrace this teaching of Jesus?*

_____

_____

_____

_____

_____

_____

_____

"We're in a rebuilding phase," says one man. This seems like a positive spin on a dire situation. I don't know what to say. *How do we know when to push on and when to give up? What role does God play in this?*

_____

_____

_____

_____

_____

_____

_____

Though not dynamic in delivery, our speaker's words resonate with me as he teaches from Acts 2. *How can we turn our attention from wanting to hear an eloquent speaker to remaining open to God's leading, regardless of his messenger's skill?*

From a human standpoint, the future of this church is bleak, but with the Holy Spirit anything can happen, just as it did in Acts chapter two. *How must we shift our focus from what we can do to what God can do?*

CHURCH #35: A WELL-KEPT SECRET

This church didn't come up in our online search or in the local directory of churches. We stumbled upon them while driving to another church.

Once we know their name, we find their Facebook page, confirming their location but nothing else. Their denomination's website gives service times but no contact information. We head off to church without confirming the service time or if they're even meeting. *How easy is it for people to learn about your church?*

_____

_____

_____

_____

_____

_____

_____

_____

We arrive seven minutes early, but everyone's seated and singing. My impulse is to retreat. Instead we slink in and sit. The song ends and absolutely nothing happens for several minutes. We squirm in awkward silence. *What do you do when your church service makes people want to leave?*

_____

_____

_____

_____

_____

_____

_____

_____

The Communion liturgy addresses the bread and wine, but they only share the bread and skip the cup. I feel cheated. *Which of your practices confuse visitors? How can you address this?*

_____

_____

_____

_____

_____

_____

_____

_____

_____

Only after the service does anyone talk to us. Up to this point, they'd been stoic. Now they're friendly. *Do people think your church is friendly? How can you be more engaging?*

_____

_____

_____

_____

_____

_____

_____

_____

CHURCH #36: THE SURPRISE

We walk inside to an empty lobby and head toward an amplified sound. We slink into a back row. Sunday school must be running late.

The speaker acknowledges the presence of visitors. He apologizes that there will be no service today. Their minister had an emergency, and they cancelled church. *If you cancel your service, how can you accommodate the people who show up?*

Sunday school ends, and the people leave. A woman apologizes for their cancelled service. She shares her faith journey. Her pilgrimage encourages me. *How ready are you to share your spiritual journey? What can you do to be better prepared?*

This is an apostolic church, with Spirit-filled members. I wonder why they didn't rely on the Holy Spirit to help them hold their service. *What would you need to do to have church without your minister?*

Though a typical church service didn't occur, fellowship did. We proclaimed Jesus, worshiped the Father, and celebrated the Holy Spirit—all without music or message. Today may be one of our best Sundays yet. *What elements must exist for church to happen? How can you provide them when the unexpected occurs?*

CHURCH #37: ANOTHER SMALL CHURCH

This church looks abandoned. With only two other cars, today promises to be another tiny gathering.

The interior offers nothing to counter my gloomy assessment. A missing ceiling tile in the entryway reveals a giant cobweb moving at the whim of the wind that enters with us. I think something is falling, and I duck. *Look at your church building carefully. What must you clean, fix, or update?*

We open the hymnal to the announced page, but the words are wrong. We've never heard the song and can't participate. We stand mute while others sing with abandon. We later discover they have two hymnals. *What do members know that guests might not?*

For the rest of the songs they use an overhead projector to display the words. One of the teens switches out the transparencies, a role he takes seriously. *How can you involve young people—the future of your church—in your service?*

_____

_____

_____

_____

_____

_____

_____

_____

The preacher's over-amplified speech reverberates throughout the sanctuary, making his message more akin to yelling. I sense a headache coming on. *What steps can you take so that the audiovisual part of your service aids the experience and doesn't distract from it?*

_____

_____

_____

_____

_____

_____

_____

_____

CHURCH #38: A REFRESHING TIME

The church meets in a middle school's all-purpose room. Large portable signs direct us to the entrance.

People mill about: talking, sipping coffee, or munching snacks. They represent all age groups, with many kids. *Younger people are the future of our church. What can you do to attract and connect with them?*

_____

_____

_____

_____

_____

_____

_____

A team of four leads worship, with optimally adjusted audio. The ideal sound tech is the one you're unaware of. It's only because of mistakes that anyone usually notices. This one is good. *What should you do to make sure your audiovisual team supports your service and doesn't distract?*

_____

_____

_____

_____

_____

_____

_____

As a special treat, three ladies from a local ballet company worship with us in dance. Ballet and guitars are an odd pairing, but the result is worshiping God through sound and movement. *What fresh worship experiences can you add to your service?*

_____

_____

_____

_____

_____

_____

_____

Our leader gives us the freedom to dance—or not. I don't have a danceable bone in my body, so I appreciate the permission to stay still, yet I'm disappointed because only a few join in. *Worshipful dance occurs in the Bible. How can you incorporate dance into your church service?*

_____

_____

_____

_____

_____

_____

_____

_____

CHURCH #39: A GREAT WAY TO END THE YEAR

With Sunday falling between Christmas and New Year's Day, I have low expectations.

Yet inside, friendly faces and hearty handshakes greet us. People acknowledge us as first-timers, without fawning over us. *How can you better embrace newcomers without making them uncomfortable?*

We slide into the fifth row, which is also the back row. I'm dismayed over the pews' lack of lumbar support. I squirm throughout the service and soon have a terrible backache. *What can you do to make sure your seating doesn't distract people from encountering God?*

The congregation recites this week's memory verse in unison. The pastor then challenges them to recall last week's verse, which he leads them in saying. *What can you do to help people hide God's word in their hearts (Psalm 119:11)?*

_____

_____

_____

_____

_____

_____

_____

They invite us to a fast food restaurant after church. When we sit, no one joins us. It's awkward until a lady moves to our booth midway through the meal. It only takes one person to make the difference between feeling seen or ignored. *What can you do to help others feel accepted?*

_____

_____

_____

_____

_____

_____

_____

CHURCH #40: NO TIME TO RETURN

Our destination is a church we've heard of often but know little about. Our favorable impressions suggest a thriving, dynamic congregation. After the service they invite us back. I want to say yes, but our schedule won't permit it.

As we walk inside, a young man introduces us to his wife, and they invite us to sit with them. We gladly accept his visitor-friendly outreach. *What can you do to help visitors feel more welcomed and comfortable?*

_____

_____

_____

_____

_____

_____

_____

Avoiding the often-awkward greeting time, they pass a friendship pad for everyone to sign. It contains a visitor card, which Candy completes, but she doesn't know what to do with it. They solved one problem but created another. *How can you make your expectations clearer?*

_____

_____

_____

_____

_____

_____

_____

Foremost in their church vision is prayer. "There is power in prayer," states the preacher. "Prayer should be our default inclination." *How can you make prayer a more significant part of your church service and your faith?*

After the service, our seatmates give us a tour of the facility. What an inclusive gesture. I feel honored. *How can you better include, accept, and honor guests?*

CHURCH #41: PEOPLE MAKE THE DIFFERENCE

The newer building doesn't look like a typical church. The sanctuary is open and inviting, with a comfortable feel.

"Hi, are you the DeHaans?" The usher's question surprises me. Either he looked up Candy's picture online or he assumed the new people matched the name in her email. Though this might be off-putting to some, the extra effort impresses me. *How can you honor a visitor (without going too far)?*

___

The area is in a flu epidemic. The minister gives us permission to avoid hugs and handshakes. He suggests an "elbow bump," which I'm happy to do, but most people don't follow his suggestion. *How easy is it to adjust your normal practices when there's a good reason to do so?*

Bits of liturgy occur throughout the service. The words, printed in their oversized bulletins, also appear overhead. I so appreciate this. *How can you help people better participate in your service?*

_____

_____

_____

_____

_____

_____

_____

_____

_____

Afterward we enjoy an engaging conversation with a lady as we share our faith journeys. Only later do we learn she's visiting too. *What does it say about you and your church when it's visitors who connect with other visitors? What must change?*

_____

_____

_____

_____

_____

_____

_____

_____

CHURCH #42: HIGH EXPECTATIONS AND GREAT DISAPPOINTMENT

I've heard a great deal about the minister and this church. I've wanted to visit for a long time.

Inside we weave through a throng of people, but no one acknowledges us. We're invisible. Do they even care about newcomers, or are they too big to notice? *How much do your actions show you care about visitors?*

_____

_____

_____

_____

_____

_____

_____

_____

The service is a copy of a church we attended thirty-five years ago. Then it was exciting. Now it's tired. I'm painfully disappointed. *What do you need to change in your service to stay fresh and relevant?*

_____

_____

_____

_____

_____

_____

_____

_____

We learn that doctrine is important to them. Though the teaching seems grounded in scripture, the minister makes divisive claims not found in the text, which he delivers with dogmatic passion. *Does your doctrine divide the church of Jesus or unify it? What needs to change?*

_____

_____

_____

_____

_____

_____

_____

In his sermon, the minister criticizes "heretical charismatic ministers." Though he might be referring to specific charismatic teachers, I infer he thinks all charismatic leaders are heretics. It's human nature to vilify what we don't understand. *How can you better embrace people who hold different views than you?*

_____

_____

_____

_____

_____

_____

_____

CHURCH #43: A WELCOMING CHURCH WITH MUCH TO OFFER

Located in a building with shared tenant space, this church has an inviting location, easily accessible, with nearby parking.

With little room to mingle, we sit down. Several people come over to greet us. They give a heartfelt thanks for visiting and invite us back. *How can you engage with people who sit in silence waiting for the service to begin?*

We've identified two key elements that make us feel truly welcomed at churches. One is sharing names, and the other is making a connection. Any attempt works, provided it doesn't become an interrogation. *How can you do better at connecting with others?*

Their multipage bulletin contains their liturgy, but I get my pages out of order and later joke about my ineptitude to an elderly man. "We *have* to get a projector to display the words," he says. "I've wanted this for years." *How can technology make your service more accessible?*

_____
_____
_____
_____
_____
_____
_____
_____

Except for the prayer and message, the members handle the service. *How much of your service do leaders handle and how much do members take care of? What can you do to allow for more participation?*

_____
_____
_____
_____
_____
_____
_____
_____

CHURCH #44: A FAMILIAR PLACE

We attended this church years ago. This won't be a visit as much as a reunion.

The building is twenty-five years old and well-maintained. Too many church buildings show neglect, repelling people instead of inviting them. *What are some low-cost ways you can upgrade the appearance of your church facility?*

_____

_____

_____

_____

_____

_____

_____

_____

The worship team has a full sound, upbeat and energetic, yet most of the congregation stands stoic. They're spectators. *How can you be an example to encourage others to participate more fully in worship?*

_____

_____

_____

_____

_____

_____

_____

_____

Without a pulpit, the pastor moves to a tall table with two chairs, giving a coffee shop vibe. He introduces today's topic, and then takes a dramatic pause while taking a sip of tea. He's not preaching a sermon, as much as having a conversation. *How can your church service better connect with today's audience? What will you say to those who don't like the change?*

The sermon is about our creed. The minister concludes by asking two questions: "What do you believe?" and "How are you living it out?" *How do you live out your faith?*

PART THREE PERSPECTIVE

As we wind up this phase of our journey, our experiences are starting to blur. Yes, I still notice kindnesses offered and innovations presented, but I worry I'm now more apt to notice the negative. I pray against that.

I've noted the importance of community. Some churches excel at it, a few fail, and most fall in-between. *How can your church do better at providing community?*

_____
_____
_____
_____
_____
_____
_____
_____

Integral to community is greeting. Greeting well fosters community. It happens before the service, during any official greeting time within the service, and afterward. *How can you greet more effectively?*

_____
_____
_____
_____
_____
_____
_____
_____

THE HOME STRETCH

Our journey is winding down.

Visiting churches has been insightful, but our exploration has worn on us too. We carry both attitudes. Similarly, each person at your church comes with baggage and something they want to achieve or escape. *How can you better meet the needs of others? (Hint, it starts with talking to them.)*

___

Though you'd think I'd find visiting churches easy by now, I'm still anxious each week. So, too, is every visitor to your church. *What can you do to help people feel less anxious and more embraced?*

CHURCH #45: ANOTHER DOUBLEHEADER

Today we'll enjoy another doubleheader: a traditional service followed by a contemporary one.

As we wander inside, several people acknowledge our presence, thanking us for visiting. But beyond that no one says anything more, so we meander into the sanctuary. *Acknowledging a person is a great start, but what more can you do to connect with them and show you care?*

_____

_____

_____

_____

_____

_____

_____

At one point, the minister invites people to come forward to the altar. Doing this in the middle of the service is unusual, and I don't catch the purpose. *When you do something people don't expect, how can you make your intentions clear?*

_____

_____

_____

_____

_____

_____

_____

Between services is a pastor's breakfast for guests. They say it's in the library but fail to explain how to get there. Eventually someone gives us directions. *How can you help people better navigate your facility?*

_____

_____

_____

_____

_____

_____

_____

_____

The crowd is lethargic at the contemporary service. It's as though they just crawled out of bed and rolled into church—and many rolled in late. *What must you do to engage in worship? How can you help others in their worship?*

_____

_____

_____

_____

_____

_____

_____

_____

CHURCH #46: FALSE ASSUMPTIONS

The sprawling facility provides an impressive view from a distance. Their larger, new building suggests a thriving, dynamic community.

Yet no one responds to Candy's phone messages or emails, so she can't confirm the service time listed on their website. As we pull up, doubt forms. Only a few cars sit in their large parking lot. Are we here at the wrong time? *How can you better respond to those who contact your church?*

_____

_____

_____

_____

_____

_____

_____

_____

During worship, heavily orchestrated background tracks reverberate through the sanctuary. I can't push past the overproduced, resounding boom. It distracts me from the words and blocks my worship. *How can you best help people worship God?*

_____

_____

_____

_____

_____

_____

_____

_____

The pastor tells the congregation to open their Bibles and follow along as he reads. The verses don't appear on the screens. With our version not matching his, it's disconcerting. I feel marginalized and excluded. *What changes do you need to make to help guests feel included?*

The minister is a gifted communicator. I appreciate his teaching about church discipline. He soon wins me over. He says that we cannot judge the lost, but we do need to judge ourselves. *Are you wrongly judgmental? What needs to change?*

CHURCH #47: SIGNIFICANT INTERACTIONS

My pre-church prayer seems mired in the rut of routine. So it is when we pray this morning and head out for today's church.

When Candy confirmed the time for this church, they invited us to arrive early for coffee. I would have stayed afterward, but to come early is more awkward than I'm willing to endure. *How can you make sure your efforts at connection are easy for people to accept?*

___

With everyone ignoring us when we arrive, we sit. A woman comes up and tells us what to expect during the service, including communion. No one in forty-six churches has done this. *How can you help visitors feel at ease and know what to expect?*

Today is the first time on our journey where I'm free to focus on the moment of Communion and not worry about the method. *What can you do to help others better engage in your service and encounter God?*

___

After the service a man greets us and asks how he can pray for us. This is another first on our journey. I so appreciate his offer. *In what ways can you be available and ready to pray for others?*

CHURCH #48: SMALL, SIMPLE, AND SATISFYING

The church's pastor is out of town, and the laity leads the entire service.

Someone asks us to sign their guestbook but then scrambles to find a pen. Though once common, guestbooks now seem archaic and carry privacy concerns. *What practices do you need to change because they no longer fit today's culture?*

_____

_____

_____

_____

_____

_____

_____

_____

A friend invites us to sit with her and her husband. The leader gives some announcements and then asks for more. After others share, our friend stands and introduces us to the crowd. It's a nice gesture. *How can you introduce new people to others and thereby reduce their discomfort?*

_____

_____

_____

_____

_____

_____

_____

_____

After a song they offer "prayers for the people." The leader opens and then pauses. After a bit of silence, someone else prays, and a few more follow. I like their approach, effectively sharing with each other as they talk to God. *How can you make group prayer more meaningful and less awkward?*

Afterward we stay for coffee and cookies. We linger for forty-five minutes before heading home, happy for our time at church today. *What should you change so that people want to tarry and enjoy Christian community?*

CHURCH #49: LARGE AND ANONYMOUS

This church is huge, the largest so far.

I wonder if I'll find a space in their packed parking lot and fight off the urge to flee in panic. Large churches need parking attendants. *What can you do to help people find a place to park and not drive away?*

The large lobby has hundreds of people milling about. Just inside, a man approaches us. He's wearing an ear mic. I wonder if he's the pastor, but he simply introduces himself as John. Unfortunately, he's the only one to talk to us. *What can you do to greet visitors?*

Candy spots a coat rack and we head toward it. It's full, and so is the next one. The third one has room. Just as it's hospitable to leave spaces for visitors to park near the entrance, leave space in the coat racks too. *How can you make room for guests?*

___

During his message, John instructed members to look for visitors to greet. But no one makes any effort, not even the man sitting in front of us who wears a deacon nametag. He looks past us. *What can you do next Sunday to better greet people you don't know?*

CHURCH #50: SATURDAY MASS

few months ago, we went to church on Saturday morning. Now we head off for a Saturday evening mass.

The worship leader directs us to "page one in the white book," but what we find doesn't match what they say. We're confused and can't follow along. *How can you make it easier for people to participate in your service?*

_____

_____

_____

_____

_____

_____

_____

_____

For the Eucharist, the priest says nothing about nonmembers, though I know we're excluded. Still, I can have the spiritual encounter of Holy Communion without physically taking part. *How can you serve Communion in a way that includes everyone?*

_____

_____

_____

_____

_____

_____

_____

_____

The tradition of sharing the chalice still disgusts us. Most participants receive the wafer and bypass the cup. I suppose some must avoid alcohol, while for others it's a sanitary issue. *What traditions should you change to address the concerns of today's visitors?*

___

___

___

___

___

___

___

___

Afterward I chat briefly with the priest. He knows we're visiting but doesn't ask our names. This might be because a member hovers about, anxious to talk to him. Though I don't feel slighted, many people would. *What behaviors do you need to change to be more visitor-focused?*

___

___

___

___

___

___

___

___

CHURCH #51: THE MEGACHURCH: A GRAND AND WELCOMING EXPERIENCE

I'm both excited and apprehensive about visiting our area's largest church.

A sign at their drive tells first-time visitors to turn on their four-way flashers—because they want to give us VIP treatment. I don't bother and follow the flow of cars, but it's a nice touch. *What can you do to give visitors VIP treatment?*

___

After the opening set, one of the co-pastors explains that it's nametag Sunday, something new they're trying to facilitate better connections with one another. *How can you help people connect with each other?*

___

After the service I turn in our visitor card and they offer a tour of the facility. Our guide wraps up with a challenge to come back for three months to see how our faith grows. "You can't evaluate a church on just one visit." *How can you encourage others on their faith journey?*

_____

_____

_____

_____

_____

_____

_____

While making connection was a concern at Church #50, forming meaningful friendships would be even harder here. But they do offer opportunities to meet people and form deeper relationships on Sunday nights and throughout the week. *How can you help people connect at your church?*

_____

_____

_____

_____

_____

_____

_____

CHURCH #52: PLAYING IT SAFE

Our destination is not a church to visit but a revisit, returning to the congregation we were part of a decade ago.

This church would be bigger, except they keep sending members away to plant new churches. *How could your church do better at sending people into the world to advance God's kingdom?*

_____
_____
_____
_____
_____
_____
_____

After the service the pastor invites people to come forward for prayer with the prayer teams. I appreciate them serving people through prayer, but few churches do. Don't they see prayer as important? *How can you elevate prayer at your church?*

_____
_____
_____
_____
_____
_____
_____

Today we heard an insightful message from a gifted communicator. We enjoyed worship led by talented musicians. Yet something felt off. They have a traditional soul. "Safe" best describes their vibe. *How can you help move your church from playing it safe to being bold for Jesus?*

I had meaningful conversations today, but they were all with people I knew. If I had shown up as a stranger, I would have departed as a stranger, feeling more alone than when I had arrived. *What can you do to make sure no one leaves your church feeling like a stranger?*

CHURCH #53: HOME FOR HOLY WEEK

It's Easter and we're returning home to our church, the people we love and miss. This marks our first Sunday here since last Easter.

There's nothing special about the building, except that it's 150 years old. Even with many enhancements, a dated look pervades. *What updates does your church need so that it doesn't feel dated?*

_____

_____

_____

_____

_____

_____

_____

_____

The pastor welcomes everyone, telling visitors what the regulars already know: there's no plan for the service, only a general intent. Its length is unknown. It will end when it ends. *How should you better depend on the Holy Spirit to guide your church service?*

_____

_____

_____

_____

_____

_____

_____

_____

The worship team launches into song, with worship at its passionate finest, full of joy and abounding in celebration. People on stage jump and dance, with more movement in the congregation than I've seen in a long time. *What does God think about your worship? How can you worship him better?*

_____

_____

_____

_____

_____

_____

_____

They baptize several people. For many churches, baptism is a somber affair, conducted with reserved formality. Not so here. It's a celebration of unabashed enthusiasm, with the congregation cheering each baptism. *How can you move baptism from a religious rite to the spiritual rebirth that it represents?*

_____

_____

_____

_____

_____

_____

_____

PART FOUR PERSPECTIVE

To wrap up our adventure, we picked churches to provide the most varied experiences. For this phase my thoughts center on church size, coupled with my desire for community.

Community is easier at smaller churches, yet I don't go to one. Curious. *Regardless of the size of your church, how can you better connect people in community?*

___

Smaller churches are usually older congregations. They often have traditional services, don't embrace newer methods, and are mostly composed of aging parishioners. I'm not against older people, but I am against complacency. *How can you guard against complacency?*

___

REFLECTIONS

Our journey of visiting fifty-two churches is over, though the memories will last forever.

I hope the questions in this book have spurred a lot of great ideas. But without action, great ideas amount to nothing. *What are the top three things you want to start doing differently?*

_____

_____

_____

_____

_____

_____

_____

_____

In visiting churches, one person often made the difference between us feeling accepted and rejected. *In addition to changes you want to make in your own interactions with visitors, how can you encourage others to follow your example?*

_____

_____

_____

_____

_____

_____

_____

_____

A LOT LIKE DATING

Visiting churches seems a lot like dating.

Church websites and social media pages are like a dating profile, with the best photos—sometimes out-of-date or misleading—and featuring positive traits while ignoring flaws. *What changes should you make online and in printed materials to present an accurate representation of your church?*

_____

_____

_____

_____

_____

_____

_____

_____

If visiting a church is like dating, joining a church might correspond to marriage. When you join a church, you commit and stop seeing other churches. *What can you do to help first-timers return, form meaningful connections, and commit to your faith community?*

_____

_____

_____

_____

_____

_____

_____

_____

GREETING WELL OR NOT AT ALL

Too often one person made the difference between us feeling welcomed or ignored, forming our perceptions of the church. Greeting occurs before, during, and after the service.

The 52 Churches Workbook

The pre-service greeting forms a first impression, while a post-service greeting provides the impression people leave with. *How can you better engage with visitors before and after your service?*

_____

_____

_____

_____

_____

_____

_____

With interaction during the service it's critical to address people you don't know. Then introduce them to your friends. *How can you interact with visitors more effectively during the service to help them feel welcomed?*

_____

_____

_____

_____

_____

_____

_____

_____

FORMAT AND SIZE MATTERS

In general, we found smaller churches offered more opportunity to make connections. We also discovered that most liturgical churches weren't very friendly.

Churches have characteristics that often relate to their size. *How can you tap the strengths of your church's size and counter its weaknesses to better connect with others?*

_____

_____

_____

_____

_____

_____

_____

_____

The format of a church's service and the practices of members also impact the likelihood of embracing visitors. *Given your church's characteristics in these areas, what changes should you embrace to better welcome guests?*

_____

_____

_____

_____

_____

_____

_____

_____

CANDY'S TAKE ON 52 CHURCHES

What an adventure! We had the honor of worshipping with friends, old and new. Here are two key points:

The most important thing I (Candy) learned from this trek was how to—and how not to—make someone feel welcome. *How can you better reach out to visitors and those you don't recognize?*

_____
_____
_____
_____
_____
_____
_____
_____

The church is the body of Christ, not a single congregation or just one denomination. We have a huge spiritual family, with varied practices. *How should you adjust your understanding of church and Christianity to better embrace its vastness and diversity?*

_____
_____
_____
_____
_____
_____
_____
_____

GENERALIZATIONS

Stating generalities is risky, but it is a way of processing information. Here are two:

Churches with older congregations and traditional services tended to be friendlier than contemporary services with younger people. *Does your church match this observation or break from it? What must change?*

_____
_____
_____
_____
_____
_____
_____
_____

I'm dismayed that we witnessed dogmatic, closed-minded, and exclusive attitudes at some churches. *If your church produces division, what can you do to promote unity?*

_____
_____
_____
_____
_____
_____
_____
_____

TIPS FOR IMPROVEMENT

We witnessed more than a few oversights, errors, and blunders that could turn people away. Sadly, many occurred in more than one church. Here are some pointers to consider so you don't scare away guests.

Realtors stress curb appeal. So should churches. *What can you do to make the outside of your building inviting? How can you ensure the inside continues the positive experience?*

_____

_____

_____

_____

_____

_____

_____

Having an online presence is critical to attract new people. Short of a personal invitation, most people won't visit a church that lacks an inviting online presence. *What steps can you take to invite people to your church?*

_____

_____

_____

_____

_____

_____

_____

People attend a church for the service. Make it easy for everyone to participate. *What can you personally do to help newcomers better understand and take part in your service?*

___

To remain viable for the long term, a church needs to look outside themselves. Too many churches have an internal focus. *What outward-looking initiatives could you pursue?*

___

CONCLUSION

Everyone was intrigued when we told them about our journey. They wanted to hear more.

Most people admitted they could never embark on such a bold quest and certainly not for a full year. When a new person walks into your church, imagine how many churches they might have already visited. *What can you do to help them find a church home?*

I hope readers will have a renewed sense of how diverse Christianity is. *How can you expand your view of what it means to be a Christian and follow Jesus?*

THE VISITING CHURCHES SERIES

Which book do you want to read next in the Visiting Churches Series?

- 52 Churches
- More Than 52 Churches
- Visiting Online Church
- Shopping for Church
- The More Than 52 Churches Workbook

ABOUT PETER DEHAAN

Peter DeHaan, PhD, wants to change the world one word at a time. His books and blog posts discuss God, the Bible, and church, geared toward spiritual seekers and church dropouts. Many people feel church has let them down, and Peter seeks to encourage them as they search for a place to belong.

But he's not afraid to ask tough questions or make religious people squirm. He's not trying to be provocative. Instead, he seeks truth, even if it makes people uncomfortable. Peter urges Christians to push past the status quo and reexamine how they practice their faith in every part of their lives.

Peter earned his doctorate, awarded with high distinction, from Trinity College of the Bible and Theological Seminary. He lives with his wife in beautiful Southwest Michigan and wrangles crossword puzzles in his spare time.

A lifelong student of Scripture, Peter wrote the 1,000-page website ABibleADay.com to encourage people to explore the Bible, the greatest book ever written. His popular blog, at PeterDeHaan.com, addresses biblical Christianity to build a faith that matters.

Read his blog, receive his newsletter, and learn more at PeterDeHaan.com.

BOOKS BY PETER DEHAAN

Visiting Churches Series

52 Churches

The 52 Churches Workbook

More Than 52 Churches

The More Than 52 Churches Workbook

Visiting Online Church

Shopping for Church

40-Day Bible Study Series

Dear Theophilus (the Gospel of Luke)

Acts Bible Study

Isaiah Bible Study

Minor Prophets Bible Study

Job Bible Study

Living Water (John)

Love Is Patient (1 and 2 Corinthians)

Revelation Bible Study

1, 2, & 3 John Bible Study

Hebrews Bible Study

James and Jude Bible Study

Matthew Bible Study

1 & 2 Peter Bible Study

Mark Bible Study

Holiday Celebration Devotionals

The Advent of Jesus

The Passion of Jesus (Lent)

The Victory of Jesus (Easter)

The Ministry of Jesus

Thanksgiving with Jesus

New Year with Jesus

Bible Character Sketches Series

Women of the Bible

The Friends and Foes of Jesus

Old Testament Sinners and Saints

More Old Testament Sinners and Saints

Heroes and Heavies of the Apocrypha

200 Old Testament Sinners and Saints

Other Books

Elephant God

Jesus's Broken Church

Martin Luther's 95 Theses (formerly *95 Tweets*)

The Christian Church's LGBTQ Failure

Bridging the Sacred-Secular Divide (formerly *Woodpecker Wars*)

Beyond Psalm 150

How Big Is Your Tent?

For the latest list of all Peter's books, go to PeterDeHaan.com/books.

www.ingramcontent.com/pod-product-compliance
Lightning Source LLC
Chambersburg PA
CBHW072007110526
44592CB00012B/1230